GW00363334

Francis Frith's
AROUND GUILDFORD

PHOTOGRAPHIC MEMORIES

Francis Frith's
AROUND GUILDFORD

◆

Keith Howell

THE FRANCIS FRITH COLLECTION

FRITH
BOOK Co

First published in the United Kingdom in 2000 by
Frith Book Company Ltd

British Library Cataloguing in Publication Data

Around Guildford
Keith Howell
ISBN 1-85937-117-5

Frith Book Company Ltd
Frith's Barn, Teffont,
Salisbury, Wiltshire SP3 5QP
Tel: +44 (0) 1722 716 376
Email: info@frithbook.co.uk
www.frithbook.co.uk

Printed and bound in Great Britain

*The author would like to thank the staff
at the Surrey History Centre in Woking
for their kind assistance*

Front Cover: High Street 1903 50869

CONTENTS

Francis Frith: Victorian Pioneer 7

Frith's Archive - A Unique Legacy 10

Around Guildford - An Introduction 12

The Heart of Guildford 15

The Castle 41

Around The Town 47

The Environs 61

Along the River Wey 68

Index 83

Free Mounted Print Voucher 87

FRANCIS FRITH: *Victorian Pioneer*

FRANCIS FRITH, Victorian founder of the world-famous photographic archive, was a complex and multitudinous man. A devout Quaker and a highly successful Victorian businessman, he was both philosophic by nature and pioneering in outlook.

By 1855 Francis Frith had already established a wholesale grocery business in Liverpool, and sold it for the astonishing sum of £200,000, which is the equivalent today of over £15,000,000. Now a multi-millionaire, he was able to indulge his passion for travel. As a child he had pored over travel books written by early explorers, and his fancy and imagination had been stirred by family holidays to the sublime mountain regions of Wales and Scotland. 'What a land of spirit-stirring and enriching scenes and places!' he had written. He was to return to these scenes of grandeur in later years to 'recapture the thousands of vivid and tender memories', but with a different purpose. Now in his thirties, and captivated by the new science of photography, Frith set out on a series of pioneering journeys to the Nile regions that occupied him from 1856 until 1860.

INTRIGUE AND ADVENTURE

He took with him on his travels a specially-designed wicker carriage that acted as both dark-room and sleeping chamber. These far-flung journeys were packed with intrigue and adventure. In his life story, written when he was sixty-three, Frith tells of being held captive by bandits, and of fighting 'an awful midnight battle to the very point of surrender with a deadly pack of hungry, wild dogs'. Sporting flowing Arab costume, Frith arrived at Akaba by camel seventy years before Lawrence, where he encountered 'desert princes and rival sheikhs, blazing with jewel-hilted swords'.

During these extraordinary adventures he was assiduously exploring the desert regions bordering the Nile and patiently recording the antiquities and peoples with his camera. He was the first photographer to venture beyond the sixth cataract. Africa was still the mysterious 'Dark Continent', and Stanley and Livingstone's historic meeting was a decade into the future. The conditions for picture taking confound belief. He laboured for hours in his wicker dark-room in the sweltering heat of the desert, while the volatile chemicals fizzed dangerously in their trays. Often he was forced to work in remote tombs and caves

where conditions were cooler. Back in London he exhibited his photographs and was 'rapturously cheered' by members of the Royal Society. His reputation as a photographer was made overnight. An eminent modern historian has likened their impact on the population of the time to that on our own generation of the first photographs taken on the surface of the moon.

VENTURE OF A LIFE-TIME

Characteristically, Frith quickly spotted the opportunity to create a new business as a specialist publisher of photographs. He lived in an era of immense and sometimes violent change. For the poor in the early part of Victoria's reign work was a drudge and the hours long, and people had precious little free time to enjoy themselves.

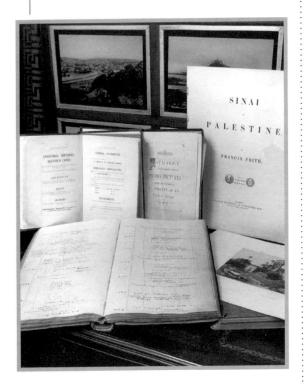

Most had no transport other than a cart or gig at their disposal, and had not travelled far beyond the boundaries of their own town or village. However, by the 1870s, the railways had threaded their way across the country, and Bank Holidays and half-day Saturdays had been made obligatory by Act of Parliament. All of a sudden the ordinary working man and his family were able to enjoy days out and see a little more of the world.

With characteristic business acumen, Francis Frith foresaw that these new tourists would enjoy having souvenirs to commemorate their days out. In 1860 he married Mary Ann Rosling and set out with the intention of photographing every city, town and village in Britain. For the next thirty years he travelled the country by train and by pony and trap, producing fine photographs of seaside resorts and beauty spots that were keenly bought by millions of Victorians. These prints were painstakingly pasted into family albums and pored over during the dark nights of winter, rekindling precious memories of summer excursions.

THE RISE OF FRITH & CO

Frith's studio was soon supplying retail shops all over the country. To meet the demand he gathered about him a small team of photographers, and published the work of independent artist-photographers of the calibre of Roger Fenton and Francis Bedford. In order to gain some understanding of the scale of Frith's business one only has to look at the catalogue issued by Frith & Co in 1886: it runs to some 670

pages, listing not only many thousands of views of the British Isles but also many photographs of most European countries, and China, Japan, the USA and Canada – note the sample page shown above from the hand-written *Frith & Co* ledgers detailing pictures taken. By 1890 Frith had created the greatest specialist photographic publishing company in the world, with over 2,000 outlets – more than the combined number that Boots and WH Smith have today! The picture on the right shows the *Frith & Co* display board at Ingleton in the Yorkshire Dales. Beautifully constructed with mahogany frame and gilt inserts, it could display up to a dozen local scenes.

POSTCARD BONANZA

◆

The ever-popular holiday postcard we know today took many years to develop. In 1870 the Post Office issued the first plain cards, with a pre-printed stamp on one face. In 1894 they allowed other publishers' cards to be sent through the mail with an attached adhesive halfpenny stamp. Demand grew rapidly, and in 1895 a new size of postcard was permitted called the

court card, but there was little room for illustration. In 1899, a year after Frith's death, a new card measuring 5.5 x 3.5 inches became the standard format, but it was not until 1902 that the divided back came into being, with address and message on one face and a full-size illustration on the other. *Frith & Co* were in the vanguard of postcard development, and Frith's sons Eustace and Cyril continued their father's monumental task, expanding the number of views offered to the public and recording more and more places in Britain, as the coasts and countryside were opened up to mass travel.

Francis Frith died in 1898 at his villa in Cannes, his great project still growing. The archive he created continued in business for another seventy years. By 1970 it contained over a third of a million pictures of 7,000 cities, towns and villages. The massive photographic record Frith has left to us stands as a living monument to a special and very remarkable man.

Frith's Archive: *A Unique Legacy*

FRANCIS FRITH'S legacy to us today is of immense significance and value, for the magnificent archive of evocative photographs he created provides a unique record of change in 7,000 cities, towns and villages throughout Britain over a century and more. Frith and his fellow studio photographers revisited locations many times down the years to update their views, compiling for us an enthralling and colourful pageant of British life and character.

We tend to think of Frith's sepia views of Britain as nostalgic, for most of us use them to conjure up memories of places in our own lives with which we have family associations. It often makes us forget that to Francis Frith they were records of daily life as it was actually being lived in the cities, towns and villages of his day. The Victorian age was one of great and often bewildering change for ordinary people, and though the pictures evoke an impression of slower times, life was as busy and hectic as it is today.

We are fortunate that Frith was a photographer of the people, dedicated to recording the minutiae of everyday life. For it is this sheer wealth of visual data, the painstaking chronicle of changes in dress, transport, street layouts, buildings, housing, engineering and landscape that captivates us so much today. His remarkable images offer us a powerful link with the past and with the lives of our ancestors.

TODAY'S TECHNOLOGY

Computers have now made it possible for Frith's many thousands of images to be accessed almost instantly. In the Frith archive today, each photograph is carefully 'digitised' then stored on a CD Rom. Frith archivists can locate a single photograph amongst thousands within seconds. Views can be catalogued and sorted under a variety of categories of place and content to the immediate benefit of researchers. Inexpensive reference prints can be created for them at the touch of a mouse button, and a wide range of books and other printed materials assembled and published for a wider, more general readership - in the next twelve months over a hundred Frith local history titles will be published! The

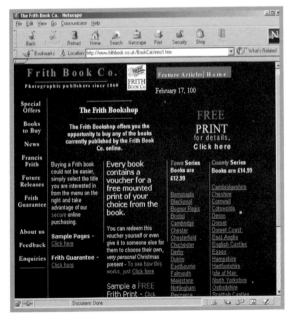

See Frith at www. frithbook.co.uk

day-to-day workings of the archive are very different from how they were in Francis Frith's time: imagine the herculean task of sorting through eleven tons of glass negatives as Frith had to do to locate a particular sequence of pictures! Yet the archive still prides itself on maintaining the same high standards of excellence laid down by Francis Frith, including the painstaking cataloguing and indexing of every view.

It is curious to reflect on how the internet now allows researchers in America and elsewhere greater instant access to the archive than Frith himself ever enjoyed. Many thousands of individual views can be called up on screen within seconds on one of the Frith internet sites, enabling people living continents away to revisit the streets of their ancestral home town, or view places in Britain where they have enjoyed holidays. Many overseas researchers welcome the chance to view special theme selections, such as transport, sports, costume and ancient monuments.

We are certain that Francis Frith would have heartily approved of these modern developments, for he himself was always working at the very limits of Victorian photographic technology.

THE VALUE OF THE ARCHIVE TODAY

Because of the benefits brought by the computer, Frith's images are increasingly studied by social historians, by researchers into genealogy and ancestory, by architects, town planners, and by teachers and schoolchildren involved in local history projects. In addition, the archive offers every one of

us a unique opportunity to examine the places where we and our families have lived and worked down the years. Immensely successful in Frith's own era, the archive is now, a century and more on, entering a new phase of popularity.

THE PAST IN TUNE WITH THE FUTURE

Historians consider the Francis Frith Collection to be of prime national importance. It is the only archive of its kind remaining in private ownership and has been valued at a million pounds. However, this figure is now rapidly increasing as digital technology enables more and more people around the world to enjoy its benefits.

Francis Frith's archive is now housed in an historic timber barn in the beautiful village of Teffont in Wiltshire. Its founder would not recognize the archive office as it is today. In place of the many thousands of dusty boxes containing glass plate negatives and an all-pervading odour of photographic chemicals, there are now ranks of computer screens. He would be amazed to watch his images travelling round the world at unimaginable speeds through network and internet lines.

The archive's future is both bright and exciting. Francis Frith, with his unshakeable belief in making photographs available to the greatest number of people, would undoubtedly approve of what is being done today with his lifetime's work. His photographs, depicting our shared past, are now bringing pleasure and enlightenment to millions around the world a century and more after his death.

AROUND GUILDFORD – *An Introduction*

THE MAJESTIC CHALK escarpment of the North Downs, running from east to west, effectively divides Surrey in two. Behind it, the ground slopes down into the Thames Valley, while in front the fertile Weald reaches towards the matching face of the South Downs. There are only two gaps in this barrier: one at Dorking, where the River Mole has carved its course en route to join the Thames at Hampton, and the other at Guildford, where the River Wey winds a similar path towards its own junction at Weybridge.

Along the crest of the Downs an ancient trackway existed long before the Roman invasion of Britain; the point where this crossed the Wey might have seemed an obvious place for a settlement. But there is no trace of such habitation until the 6th century, when pagan Saxons established a cemetery on the area of the Mount.

During the next century they were converted to Christianity, and the first written reference to the town is in the will of King Alfred in 880, when he bequeathed the royal residence to 'Glydeforda' to his nephew. This Golden Ford is probably a reference to either the sandy bed of the river at the crossing point, or to the yellow kingcups which grew on the adjoining banks.

The gradual process of expansion continued; by the closing decades of the 10th century, Guildford was established as a major trading place, minting its own silver coinage. In 1036, it is recorded as being the site of a brutal massacre of the followers of Alfred the Aytheling by Earl Godwin's men, and excavations have revealed a substantial number of mutilated skeletons buried on the Mount - these may have been among the victims of this assault. In 1050, the square flint and chalk tower of St Mary's church was constructed in what was probably the then centre of the town.

The Norman Conquest of 1066 was rapidly followed by the building of Guildford's castle: although it guarded the important river crossing, it also dominated the town itself and acted as a deterrent to any opposition from its Saxon inhabitants. The Domesday Book shows that at this time the population numbered around 700 people occupying 85 dwellings. Initially, the castle consisted of a wooden tower occupying a mound, but in 1125 it was replaced by the splendid stone keep whose remains are still such a prominent feature of the modern town. As a royal residence, the castle reached the peak of its splendour under Henry III; it had fallen into ruin and neglect by the end of the Middle Ages, although the keep itself was retained as the county gaol until 1611.

Although a comparatively small and compact settlement, the borough of Guildford was confirmed in its status as the county town by a charter in 1257; it became wealthy through its development as a major centre for the manufacture of woollen cloth, which was brought here from the surrounding countryside to be dyed and finished. This industry, which at first enhanced the town's reputation, was later damaged by the activities of some unscrupulous manufacturers; by the time of the Stuarts at the end of the 17th century, the wool trade had all but disappeared. The woolsacks incorporated into the present Borough Arms are an indication of this former prosperity.

Guildford's position on the important coaching route between London and the expanding Portsmouth naval base further enhanced its growth during this period, and the adoption in 1651 of Sir Richard Weston's scheme for the improvement of the Wey's navigation over the 15 miles between the town and the river's confluence with the Thames at Weybridge supplied a major boost to its economic well-being. Barges were now able to reach both London and Oxford from the town, making it an important centre for Surrey's flourishing corn and timber trade. The surrounding villages also fell within Guildford's commercial hinterland and helped to make the town an important and expanding centre for local commerce.

But it was the Industrial Revolution, and in particular the coming of the railway to Guildford in 1845, which prompted some of the most fundamental changes in Guildford's recent history and its overall expansion. The opportunity was now provided for prosperous, salaried employees working in London to move their families to the more salubrious

HIGH STREET 1903 50869

surroundings of the countryside, while they now commuted into the West End and the City of London. This trend, although barely noticeable at first, was further promoted and encouraged by the construction of new and extensive housing estates within easy reach of Guildford's station. As this preliminary trickle of newcomers swelled to a flood by the end of

and parking restrictions within its centre. But these changes were not only confined to transport. The centre of Guildford has also been radically altered - and many would claim despoiled - by the removal of so many of its old and much-loved buildings from previous eras and their replacement by modern architectural creations.

HIGH STREET 1935 86787

the 19th century, and the introduction of the motor vehicle gradually replaced the horse-drawn traffic of the past, Guildford and its environs were transformed, like so much of the county, from the region of agriculture, cottage industries and self-contained communities that was familiar to William Cobbett and his contemporaries.

By the closing decades of the 20th century, the area had become not only a dormitory for those working in the capital, but also a centre for new industries. The enormous growth and availability of motor transport during the second half of that same century had forced the building of new roads around the town, and the introduction of complex one-way systems

As the photographs in this volume illustrate, within the space of a mere hundred years the old face of the former county town has become barely recognisable. Ahead of us lie the increasing pressures for more change, for further sacrifices of the lingering remnants of the surrounding Surrey countryside, and for additional housing and space for expanding industries. How we, and our elected representatives, will approach the task of facing up to these increasing pressures will have to be judged by future generations; but for the moment, the pictorial contents of this volume should certainly provide food for thought.

HIGH STREET 1895 35059

This is a fine view of the steep High Street climbing up towards the Guildhall, whose famous clock can just be glimpsed beyond the massive bulk of the White Lion coaching inn on the left. The granite setts which were laid in 1868 by the borough surveyor Henry Peak are clearly apparent, and were intended to provide additional grip for horse-drawn traffic ascending the slope. On the right, the lone figure of a sandwich-board man carries advertising for Walter Clark's business.

HIGH STREET 1903 50868

As the commercial and trading centre of a large area of West Surrey, the High Street normally bustled with an assortment of carts, carriages and wagons. When motor cars first appeared on Guildford's streets the accident rate rose alarmingly, particularly amongst young children who had been used to wandering carelessly in the road.

HIGH STREET 1903 50869

The Guildhall clock is still the town's most famous landmark, and has dominated the main street since 1683, when it was donated by John Aylward in return for the freedom to set up his business in Guildford. Behind the Guildhall frontage lies the earlier hall built in the mid 16th century, with the town council's meeting chamber facing out on to the first-floor balcony. The last council meeting was held here in July 1931, before such proceedings were transferred to the municipal offices in the Upper High Street. The ground floor of the Guildhall once housed one of the town's three fire engines. The premises of Peacock and Lunn, architects, had previously been the George and Dragon pub, whilst next door, and almost under the clock, was the Guildford Arms. In 1870, the adjacent building was occupied by George Holden's Boot and Shoe Company, while next door was Shepherd the Chemist, where Mr Alex, a surgeon dentist from London, attended every Monday for the purpose of providing the painless extraction of teeth. Shepherd's was rebuilt after 1870, but was demolished in 1884 along with Holdens. A branch of the London and County Bank, later to become the National Westminster Bank, opened in their place.

MARKET STREET 1904 51858

Here we see Market Street from the High Street, with the Red
Lion pub and the Bull's Head facing each other across the
entrance. The latter is one of the few survivors of the town's
once numerous hostelries, which went into a slow decline
following the arrival of the railway in Guildford in 1845. The
Red Lion was the largest coaching inn in the town. King
Charles II was reputed to have stayed here; Samuel Pepys
certainly did in August 1668, on his way from London to
Petersfield on Admiralty business, relishing asparagus grown on
the other side of North Street. It was reduced to a pub at the
end of the 19th century, selling Crooke's ales brewed
on the far side of Town Bridge.

HIGH STREET 1908 61106
Frank Lasham took over the stationery, printing and publishing business of Andrews and Son in 1878. His major contribution to the town was the publication of the local Almanac and Directory. Next door, Wood's clothier store became Wood, White and Tucker in 1877, then Tucker and White and, by the time of this photograph, W E White. It continued in business in the High Street until 1959. Lasham's premises became Randall's shoe shop.

HIGH STREET 1909 61971
On the left is the entrance to Market Street and the
Bull's Head. On the immediate right of the picture
are the premises of Spikins & Dent, jewellers and
silversmiths. The growing popularity of photography
as a pastime is indicated by the sign above
the next door chemists.

HIGH STREET 1908 61105
The stock of W E White's clothing store is amply displayed to view in the windows of the ornately decorated premises at No 64 High Street, as a landau driven by a top-hatted coachman and footman makes its way up the hill towards the Guildhall. The store closed its doors in July 1962, and was rebuilt as a branch of Marks & Spencer.

HIGH STREET 1904 51855
This view looks down the High Street from the corner of Quarry Street, towards the Town Bridge and with the White Lion coaching inn on the right, complete with its trademark statue and flagpole above the pediment. The premises of chemists Waller Martin and Co next door, and owned at the time of this photograph by the pharmacist T L Inman, became the Astolat Tea Shoppe in 1917.

QUARRY STREET 1930 83434

Perridge's Old Blue China Shop at 104 High Street and 67 Quarry Street had become the High Street branch of W H Smith's in 1929. For most of the 19th century The Star Inn had been run by a man named Jesse Boxall: three generations of them. The first leased the pub in 1792 and ran it until 1830s, when his son, also named Jesse, took over. The third Jesse bought the premises in 1845 and was landlord until his death in 1894. The firm of Chas. Osenton were eventually replaced by Cubitt and West; but the building was occupied by estate agents and auctioneers for more than six decades. The newsvendor's placard indicates that this photograph may have been taken in the summer of 1933; this was the driest year of all between 1926 and 1979, and a period when temperatures reached the upper eighties Farenheit. Spare a thought for the poor policeman on traffic duty in his heavy tunic, helmet and white gauntlets.

QUARRY STREET 1904 51859
The young girl with her pram stands outside the shop of Thomas Hampton at 53 Quarry Street, one of a number of antique dealers who were established in the town at this time. The trees in St Mary's Churchyard on the left were removed and then replaced in later years.

STAR CORNER 1910 66803
A group of men and women gather outside Angell & Son's store on the corner of Quarry Street and the High Street around the turn of the century, with the clock on St Mary's Church showing the hour of two in the afternoon. The Star Inn was extremely popular with local carriers. Next door, the furniture store became the offices of auctioneers Chas. Osenton.

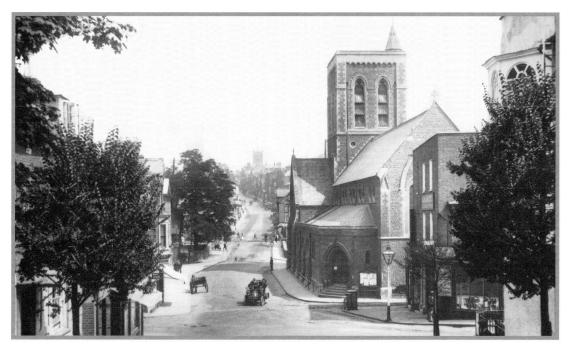

HIGH STREET 1909 61837
In this photograph the High Street is viewed from the foot of the Mount, with Bury Street and St Nicolas Church on the right, and the Town Bridge just beyond. An early motor vehicle prepares to turn right into Park Street.

HIGH STREET 1926 81413
By now the automobile had displaced the horse-drawn traffic of the past, and the coaching trade of the White Lion, with its sixty rooms, had given way to catering for motorists. Next door is the prominently advertised Astolat Tea Shoppe. To the left of the photograph, the rooftop sign for Clarks marks the premises of a music store which sold gramophones, records, pianos and pianolas.

HIGH STREET 1935 86787
Stent and Clarke's printing shop and stationers, on the
right, was once the home of the Russell family, including
the well-known painter and Royal Academician John
Russell. The building was also the office of the Surrey
Standard local paper until 1950. Next door is the major
branch of the Westminster Bank.

HIGH STREET 1936 87765

Next door to Lilley & Skinner's shoe shop is the impressive Tuscan-style portico of the old Cornmarket, built in 1818. Above the entrance are the borough arms. The corn market closed in 1901, and in 1933 the two central pillars were moved apart to allow the construction of a roadway into a new car park.

HIGH STREET c1955 G65035

Looking up the bustling High Street from the Town Bridge, this photograph offers an interesting contrast to the earlier picture from the same vantage point in 1903. The most evident changes are in the lines of parked cars, the road island and the suspended street lamp in the foreground. The gleaming, white facade of the White Lion Hotel stands out, but the rich architectural mix remains unchanged.

HIGH STREET c1955
The numerous flags and lines of bunting decorating the High Street shops and offices are in place to celebrate either the coronation of Queen Elizabeth the Second in 1953, or her official visit to the town on 27 June 1957, marking the 700th anniversary of the granting of the first Charter to the Borough of Guildford by Henry III.

HIGH STREET c1955 G65003

HIGH STREET c1955 G65002

HIGH STREET c1955 G65081

An aerial view of the centre of Guildford, taken from the tower of St Nicolas' Church, with the River Wey and the Town Bridge in the foreground. The spire of St Saviour's Church and the tower of Holy Trinity are prominent above the surrounding buildings.

HIGH STREET c1965 G65381

Modern shop frontages are much in evidence in these mid-sixties photographs, as are the increasing traffic levels and congestion.

HIGH STREET c1965 G65382
Many of the shops are branches of national retail chains, which had replaced the individual local business concerns.

HIGH STREET c1965 G65379
The Angel Hotel, which was established in the 1520s, is the only survivor of the town's five major coaching inns.

ALMS HOUSES 1895 35062

George Abbot, who was Archbishop of Canterbury from 1611 until his death in 1633, was born in Guildford in a cottage close to the Town Bridge and educated at the Grammar School. The Hospital of the Blessed Trinity was his gift of an almshouse to the town, and originally provided accommodation for twenty elderly residents when it was opened in 1622.

ABBOTS HOSPITAL c1955 G65088

In recent years Abbots Hospital has been expanded, but it remains one of Guildford's most beautiful buildings, and the best example of Tudor-style brickwork in the country.

ABBOTS HOSPITAL c1965 G65284

After the battle of Sedgemoor in July 1685, the rebellious Duke of Monmouth was brought to Guildford and housed in an upper room of the Hospital with barred windows. The Archbishop lies buried in Holy Trinity Church across the High Street.

THE GRAMMAR SCHOOL 1903 50878

Here we see the 16th-century frontage of the Grammar School, originally endowed as a charitable foundation by Robert Beckingham, a member of the Grocer's Livery Company in 1509, and set up near the Castle. In 1553 Edward VI's advisers granted the town a charter and an income for the school, and building work commenced on a plot of land just within the then town limits. Over the next thirty years the structure of brick and Horsham stone took shape, and it was finally completed in 1586.

THE GRAMMAR SCHOOL 1921 69966

The three Abbot brothers (the bishop, archbishop and Maurice, the Lord Mayor of London) were all educated here, as was Sir George Carey, the renowned colonial governor. Opposite is the entrance to Allen House, a 17th-century house with spacious grounds which, in the mid-thirties, were considered as a site for a new municipal centre. It was demolished in 1964 to make way for an expansion of the Grammar School.

NORTH STREET 1903 50873

The 135-foot spire of St Saviour's Church, built in 1899 in Woodbridge Road to replace an earlier iron church, dominates this view of North Street. On the immediate right are the County and Borough Halls. Beyond are the Congregational Hall of 1884 and the Congregational Church of 1863, which were both demolished in 1965.

NORTH STREET 1923 73384

On the left, by the ornate Victorian lamp post, are the glass walled and roofed public conveniences, popularly referred to by Guildford residents as 'the Crystal Palace'. The Theatre Royal offers a comedy production to its patrons entitled 'Our Flat'; it is publicised as being 'built for laughing purposes only' in its advertising.

NORTH STREET 1925 78116A

Some impressive vehicles await their drivers in the designated parking area on the left of the street, including a high-sided, canvas-covered, single-decker charabanc, probably built at the Woodbridge Hill works of Dennis Brothers. Their rapidly expanding factory, formed in 1901, employed a substantial number of local people in the years following the First World War.

NORTH STREET 1921 69967

A policeman stands in the doorway of the County Hall offices. Next door is the canopy over the entrance to the Theatre Royal, which had opened in the converted Borough Hall in December 1912, but which was forced to close in 1933 with the introduction of new fire regulations. It reopened as a theatre club in 1946, but was burnt down in a major fire in April 1963, and rebuilt as an extension to the Co-operative store. On the left are the fruit and vegetable stalls of the green segment of the market which moved here from Market Street in 1887, and then on to Woodbridge Road in 1896. It was re-established here after the First World War. In the absence of modern motor traffic, the stalls faced onto the open street.

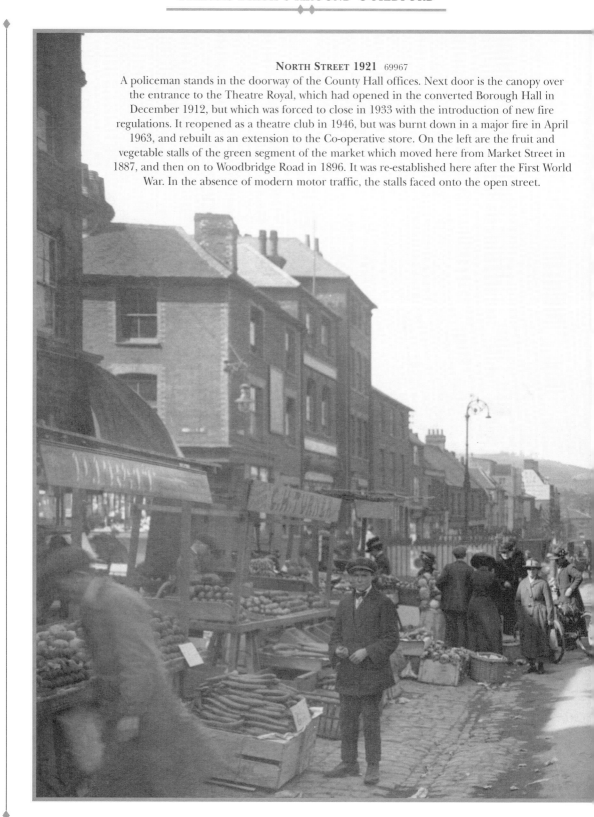

NORTH STREET 1936 87766

Behind the single-decker Green Line bus, which operated a service between Guildford and its fellow county town of Hertford, is the brick Fire Station, built in 1872. With its clock and weather vane, the twin entrances were originally arched, but these were altered at the time the horse-drawn appliances were replaced by motorised Dennis engines. On the left, the pointed pediment and balustrade mark the roof of the Borough Police Station.

NORTH STREET c1955 G65015

This view looks east up North Street towards St Saviour's Church, with the showroom of the well-known household furnishing company of John Perring's on the right. The intrusive clutter of advertising signs on the buildings was a commonplace feature of the period.

SWAN LANE c1955 G65173

SWAN LANE c1955
On the right, and with part of its signboard just visible at the top of the photograph, is the Swan Inn. This narrow thoroughfare links North Street and the High Street and, as the shopfronts and advertising signs indicate, was a popular shopping area.

ST SAVIOUR'S CHURCH c1955
The church took nine years to build, after its foundation stone was laid in 1899 by Mrs Paynter, the wife of the Reverend Francis Paynter, rector of the Guildford parish. During the final stages of its building in 1906 two intrepid individuals engaged in an unofficial contest to scale the spire. The saying, attributed to George Abbot, 'pretty Guildford, proud people, three churches, no steeple' was rendered redundant by its completion.

ST SAVIOUR'S CHURCH c1955 G65192

THE MARKET 1908 61107
All Guildford's markets were originally held in the High Street, with that for commodities being held on Saturdays and for animals on Tuesdays. The livestock market for pigs, cattle and sheep was moved to North Street in 1865, and then to this new area in Woodbridge Road in 1895.

THE MARKET 1924 75358
A bullock was purchased every week for the military personnel garrisoned at Aldershot. The last livestock market was held here at the beginning of June 1976, before transferring northwards to Slyfield Green. The new law courts and police station now occupy this site.

THE CASTLE ARCH 1904 51872
This elegant Edwardian lady, with her parasol and buttoned boots, poses on the cobblestones outside the ivy-clad cottage built by Francis Carter in 1630, which stands beside the path leading to the Castle.

THE CASTLE ARCH 1904 51871

A gardener pushes his wheelbarrow up the steep cobbled path leading from Quarry Street to the Castle. The arch was probably built by Henry III's master mason John of Gloucester in 1256 when, following a fire in 1254, the Castle was developed into a royal palace.

THE CASTLE GROUNDS, THE FISH POND 1906 54155

Three little maids from school (?) take a close interest in the water lilies and underwater residents of the fishpond, which was considerably larger then than it is today. Although the two fountains are keeping the water oxygenated, the summer heat has caused substantial evaporation, as an examination of the surrounding bank indicates.

THE CASTLE GROUNDS
The Bowling Green 1922 71759

The sedate sport of bowling has been practised here since at least 1739. In 1885, Guildford Borough Council purchased the green, along with a decrepit inn, for £2050, whilst the whole of the adjacent Castle complex, including some houses, cost only £2200. A year after this photograph was taken, the Castle Green Bowling Club was founded. The memorial to the five hundred dead of the First World War, designed by Frederick Hodgson and standing at the end of the green, was erected here in 1920. The names of a further two hundred Guildford men and women who died during the Second World War were belatedly added in November 1995.

THE CASTLE c1965 G65294

This view gives some idea of the original strategic purpose of the Castle, situated in its commanding position, as well as an excellent panoramic vista of the town in the mid-60s. Between the camera and the Castle, and slightly to the right, are the Guildford Swimming Baths. Halfway down the extreme left of the picture are the chimneys and roof of The Chestnuts, where the author and mathematician Charles Lutwidge Dodgson died on 14 January 1898. He is best known to generations of children as Lewis Carroll, the author of 'Alice's Adventures in Wonderland' and 'Alice through the Looking Glass'.

THE CASTLE 1933 85753

THE CASTLE 1933
The castle, which was built around 1070, was intended by the Normans to guard the important crossing over the River Wey. The impressive keep, with walls which are up to five metres thick in places, dates from 1125, and was built of Bargate stone quarried in the vicinity of Godalming.

THE CASTLE c1955
Purchased by the Borough Council, and opened to the public in 1888, the impressive stone keep stands on its mound with the Union flag proudly flying. To the left are the remains of the earlier shell keep, constructed from chalk.

THE CASTLE c1955 G65039

THE MILITARY HOSPITAL 1917 67923
Originally the forbidding entrance to the Guildford
Union Workhouse, which had been opened in 1838, this
solid gateway stood in Union Road (subsequently
renamed Warren Road in 1904). An infirmary had been
added in 1896 for the benefit of the sick poor of the
town. During the First World War, the buildings were used
as a military hospital; this later became Warren Road
Hospital until 1945, and then St Luke's Hospital. In latter
years it then became a radiotherapy centre and also
housed the Guildford School of Nursing, a midwifery
school and a school for radiography. The buildings were
demolished in 1965.

THE ROYAL SURREY COUNTY HOSPITAL 1936 87768

The original Royal Surrey County Hospital was opened in Farnham Road in 1866; its £17,000 cost was raised by public subscription. Dedicated to the memory of Prince Albert, and with sixty beds, it was designed as a general hospital serving not only the town but the rest of Surrey as well, and was operated along the lines of a charity for the sick poor until 1928. It then operated under a contributory scheme as the West Surrey and Aldershot Hospitals League until the National Health Service came into operation in 1948.

FARNHAM ROAD 1911 63172

The Napoleon Hotel was originally named after Emperor Napoleon III, Buonaparte's nephew, in about 1855. Next door was the shop of Miss Denton, a stationer and registry office for servants; then J Belchamber, baker; W F Parnell, a tobacconist and hairdresser, and finally the offices of W G Heath, auctioneer, estate agent and surveyor, whose prominent sign is visible above the first floor bay window. The entire block was demolished during the 1980s to make way for offices and a branch of the Young Men's Christian Association.

FARNHAM ROAD 1911 63173
Three boys in the distinctive uniform of Christ's Hospital school at Horsham walk past a group of 16th- and 17th-century cottages, 2-10 Farnham Road, which were demolished in 1957. They have probably travelled to Guildford on the Horsham to Guildford Direct Railway, which opened in 1865, and ran via Cranleigh and Bramley. The line closed in 1965 as a result of Dr Beeching's radical cutbacks to the national rail network. On the far right of the photograph are the Farnham United Breweries ale stores and offlicence.

WATERDEN ROAD 1903 50876
Originally part of the parish of Stoke-next-Guildford, Christ Church became a parish in its own right in 1936. The church had been consecrated in 1868, but its building was not completed until more than thirty years later. It has since been redecorated to plans provided by Sir Edward Maufe, the architect of Guildford cathedral, and has also undergone extensive restoration.

WESTON ROAD 1911 63178
In the suburb of Woodbridge Hill, a milkman with his churn mounted on a handcart makes his round in a street now overshadowed by the complex interchange of the modern A3 linking London and Portsmouth.

THE LIDO
Stoke Park 1933 85751
This is the pleasing result of a bold experiment to combat
unemployment in the town during the Great Depression of the
1930s. The borough council had purchased the 186-acre Stoke
Park in 1925, and in November 1932 the Mayor, William
Harvey, established a Work Fund to which all Guildford
residents were invited to contribute weekly in order to keep 700
local unemployed men occupied in building the open-air pool.
Backed up by additional funding from Whitehall, the Lido was
opened in 1933; in addition to its evident popularity with the
public, it encouraged the setting-up of similar civic projects in
Europe and North America.

THE SWIMMING POOL 1933

The summer of 1933 saw local temperatures soaring into the mid-eighties Farenheit, so these ladies' towels and costumes would probably have dried quickly in the warm atmosphere, but the provision of this modern mangle was nevertheless a much-appreciated additional amenity.

◆

CAXTON GARDENS 1911

In 1906, Billing & Sons, a major printing concern in Guildford, purchased land off Weston Road whose semi-detached houses can be seen facing the camera. The company then set up the Caxton Gardens Cottage Club, which in 1907 built a line of twenty-four modern cottages, just visible on the left, in order to provide affordable homes for its workers, at a time when rented accommodation was becoming increasingly expensive. By 1924, all the residents had purchased their properties and the scheme was terminated.

THE SWIMMING POOL 1933   G65301

CAXTON GARDENS 1911   63176

UPPER HIGH STREET 1922 71763
This view looks towards the junction of the
London Road and Epsom Road, with the small
Post Office on the right. The area has
undergone a substantial transformation in
subsequent decades, and today's shops are
positioned much further back
from the roadway.

THE CHURCH OF THE HOLY TRINITY 1927 79505

The Church of the Holy Trinity, seen here from the corner of Chertsey Street, was built in 1763 as a replacement for an original 13th-century church whose tower and steeple had collapsed in 1740. When the Guildford diocese was established in 1927, Holy Trinity became the proto-cathedral until the final consecration of the Cathedral of the Holy Spirit on Stag Hill in 1961.

UPPER HIGH STREET c1955 G65120

On the left are the old Council offices at Eastgate House, constructed in 1931. These operations moved away to their present position in the new civic offices in 1959-60. The small single-storey building at the end of the parade of shops was the former library. The White Horse hotel is just visible beyond.

UPPER HIGH STREET c1955 G65187
The White Horse Hotel is on the right, as the High Street divides into the Epsom Road and the London Road, formerly the old main coaching route of the A3 into the centre of the town.

EPSOM ROAD c1955 G65055
The mock timber frontages of the shopping parade at the start of the Epsom Road provide a backdrop for these views of shopping during the afternoon.

EPSOM ROAD c1955 G65054
Note the absence of any contemporary parking restrictions.

PORTSMOUTH ROAD 1903 50877
These elegant early Victorian houses, with their wrought iron railings and ivy-covered garden walls, stand alongside the road to Godalming.

WOODBRIDGE HILL 1911
Away from the centre of the town, the London Stores and the adjoining shops on the left would have provided a welcome alternative for local householders. The Stores offered an extensive range of household goods, as can be seen from the advertising signs. They included mantles for gas lighting, which at this time had yet to be superseded by modern domestic electricity.

YORK ROAD 1904
This view gives a good example of the widespread housing development in Guildford which ensued after the arrival of the railway in the town in 1845. These trim suburban villas were popular with commuters. Note the way the trees have been planted in the roadway itself, rather than within the pavement area. With the infant in its pram securely shaded from the summer sun, its elder sibling is accompanied by either its mother or a nanny.

WOODBRIDGE HILL 1911   63174

YORK ROAD 1904   51864

WOODBRIDGE ROAD 1906 55060
The spacious villas of Woodbridge Road, with their steeply pitched roofs and chequered brickwork facades, were built in the 1870s to meet the increasing demand for property brought about by the advent of the railways.

WOODBRIDGE ROAD 1925 76713
On the western side of the road were a number of small semi-detached houses, shops and artisan's housing.

SUTTON PLACE
South Front 1914   67044
Four miles north of Guildford, this brick and terracotta building
is one of the finest Tudor Renaissance buildings to have survived
anywhere in England; it was built in the 1520s by Sir Richard Weston,
who was later to become an Under Treasurer of England. Queen
Elizabeth the First stayed here as his guest. Sir Richard's son was
executed as a suspected lover of Anne Boleyn. Sir Richard was the
driving force behind the construction of the Wey Navigation, linking
Guildford with the Thames, and providing access to London
and Oxford. In 1960, the property was purchased by Paul Getty,
then allegedly the richest man in the world, for £400,000;
his subsequent housewarming party cost £3,500.

ON THE HOG'S BACK 1927 79576
The high, chalk spine of the Hog's Back extends from the east of Guildford towards Farnham, carrying the A31. The road is now mostly dual carriageway, but this photograph shows how narrow the road was before modern traffic demands necessitated its further development. At its summit, near the village of Puttenham, it rises to 51 metres above sea level - one of Surrey's highest points - and offers superb views across the Weald to the South Downs, and of Purbright Common and Bagshot Heath to the north.

NEWLANDS CORNER TEA ROOMS c1955 G65019
No longer in existence, this particular establishment
provided welcome refreshment to the innumerable
visitors to this famous beauty spot beside the A25 as it
leaves Guildford for Dorking. It offers extensive and
breathtaking vistas to Littlehampton, beyond the South
Downs, and to the hills into Sussex. In December 1926 it
was the scene of a major police search when the famous
novelist Agatha Christie's car was found crashed and
abandoned here. Three weeks later she was found staying
at an hotel in Harrogate, having apparently laid a false
trail following an argument with her then husband
Colonel Archibald Christie.

ST MARTHA'S CHURCH 1927 79514

Positioned in splendid isolation on a hilltop near the hamlet of Chilworth, the church is allegedly on the route of the Pilgrim's Way, which leads from Winchester to Canterbury, but the site was almost certainly previously used for heathen worship and may mark the place of a massacre of early Christian martyrs. Its name is probably derived from a corruption of the word 'martyr'.

ST MARTHA'S CHURCH c1955 G65033

The nave stands on its original Norman foundations, with the tower rising up from old piers and arches. Its first known rector was appointed around the beginning of the 13th century, when it was in the gift of nearby Newark Priory. But after the dissolution, the church fell gradually into disrepair and neglect. It suffered a further catastrophe in the 17th century, when the blast from an explosion at a gunpowder factory in Chilworth almost totally destroyed the entire building.

ST MARTHA'S CHURCH c1965 G65386

The church was restored for posterity in 1848 by a group of Surrey men, but during the First World War, because of its high visibility from the air, it was camouflaged as a clump of trees by the use of scaffolding adorned with branches. A brass inscription inside the church pays tribute to John St Loe Strachey, who resided at Newland's Corner, and founded the Spectator magazine in 1828.

THE CATHEDRAL c1965 G65383

The modern Cathedral of the Holy Spirit, standing on land at Stag Hill given by Lord Onslow of Clandon Park, can be seen from many miles around. Designed by Sir Edward Maufe, its foundation stone was laid by the Archbishop of Canterbury in July 1936 and its construction continued, though at a slow pace, throughout the Second World War. Its consecration finally took place on 22 July 1961.

KEEPER'S COTTAGE, THE CHANTRIES 1913 65227

This quaint stone cottage with its leaded windows and prominent porch, once occupied by the resident gamekeeper, still stands at the entrance to the Chantries woods near the junction of the Pilgrim's Way footpath and Shepherd's Way.

STOKE CHURCH 1895 35619

This late 15th-century church of St John the Evangelist is built of chequered flint and sandstone, with three-stage buttresses supporting its tower which houses a peal of six bells. The south-eastern turret encloses a staircase.

STOKE CHURCH 1906 55072

The church underwent much rebuilding and restoration during the 19th century; this process continued on into the 20th century, as evidenced in these photos by the replacement of the clock face.

The River Wey 1909 61845

THE RIVER WEY 1909

This tranquil scene of an Edwardian family enjoying a summer afternoon punting on the river has been cunningly posed. The photographer's camera must have been positioned almost directly beneath the bridge carrying the Guildford to Horsham railway line. The wooden gate on the extreme left is still standing across the towpath.

◆

THE RIVER WEY 1909

Further downstream, towards Guildford, another couple relaxes aboard a small skiff, with the reclining lady in the stern clearly reflected in the peaceful water. Behind them on the high cliff stands the grandiose mansion of The Beacon.

The River Wey 1909 61965

St Catherine's Chapel 1895 35073

Richard de Wauncey, the rector of St Nicholas' church, rebuilt this little chapel, a familiar landmark on its hill overlooking the River Wey, in the early 14th century. In 1308, he also obtained a licence to hold an annual fair here around the feast of St Matthew the Evangelist in October. The chapel fell into disuse in the 16th century, but the fair continued to be held up until shortly before the First World War, although attempts were made to halt it during the previous century because of concerns over a number of cholera epidemics in the vicinity. With its pinnacled buttresses, three doorways and eight large windows open to the sky, responsibility for the ruined chapel was taken over by the town in the 20th century, and the iron railings were installed to protect the remaining fabric of the building.

St Catherine's Chapel c1955 G65180

ST CATHERINE'S 1909 61696
The demure little Edwardian girl and her two male playmates in their sailor suits are being kept under the watchful eye of a lady neighbour.

St Catherine's Ferry Cottage 1909 61697

This carefully posed picture, with its reader in a straw boater seated on a stool, shows Ferry Lane running down to the River Wey bank, which can be glimpsed in the background. This is part of the Victorians' romantically named 'Pilgrim's Way'. In fact, the route was used by travellers of all descriptions long before the arrival of Christianity in Britain. Alongside the path, the water from St Catherine's Well runs down to the river. The water was reputed to have healing properties, particularly for rheumatism and eye problems.

St Catherine's Ferry 1927 79649

Walkers were ferried across the River Wey to Shalford Park aboard the broad, flat-bottomed punt seen on the left. Although the ferry service, which was important for local traffic rather than the hordes of pilgrims envisaged by the Victorians, had operated since the Middle Ages, it ceased to function in the early sixties, and was replaced by a footbridge. On 13 October 1915, a German zeppelin, possibly aiming to hit the town, dropped a premature bomb on this stretch of the river, killing an unsuspecting swan.

St Catherines 1903 50883
A plethora of metal advertising signs adorns the walls
of the village general store, which stands at the
junction of Ferry Lane and the Portsmouth Road. The
public house is still here. The sign offering
refreshment for cyclists is an indication of the
popularity of this new form of recreation around the
turn of the century.

THE RIVER WEY 1909 61841

The popularity of boating on the river in the Edwardian era is further demonstrated in this picture taken near St Catherine's, with the ferry cottage and its flat-bottomed boat moored at the landing stage clearly visible.

THE RIVER WEY, THE NEW FOOTBRIDGE 1909 61967

This wooden footbridge was built and paid for by public subscription in the year this photograph was taken. The structure, however, eventually rotted over the course of time; it has now been replaced by a stone bridge.

THE RIVER c1955 G65038

This particular locality has long been the focal point for the hiring of boats on the river. On the extreme right are the riverside gardens of the Jolly Farmer pub, whose sign hangs above the landing stage.

THE JOLLY FARMER INN 1914 66810

Here we see the frontage of the Jolly Farmer, on the left, in Shalford Road, just prior to the First World War. The pub itself dates from the previous year. The signboards for Leroy's and Allens' adjacent boathouses advertise their facilities. The cottages beyond were demolished during a road-widening scheme and the construction of the Millbrook car park.

ALLENS' BOATHOUSE 1934 86059

The boathouse, with its tea-lounge, stands supported above the river in an area notoriously prone to flooding. The covered skiffs on the right could be used for boating holidays of the kind immortalised in Jerome K. Jerome's classic comic novel 'Three Men in a Boat'.

ON THE RIVER WEY 1914 66813

Looking back upstream along this same section of the river, one has a clear view of the boat houses and the Jolly Farmer pub on the eastern bank, and the tree-shaded towpath on the west, before the Wey swings abruptly round the bend towards St Catherine's and Godalming.

THE LOCK c1955

Two intrepid couples aboard their skiff prepare to pass through the lock, watched by the inevitable group of onlookers who gather at such moments. The solitary female at the far set of gates appears to have been entrusted with overall responsibility for their safe transit. The Yvonne Arnaud Theatre now stands on the near bank.

MILL MEAD 1903

On the right is Moon's lumberyard, from whence the stacks of sawn timber were washed down onto the Town Bridge three years earlier. The height of the landing stage, and the water marks on the buildings on the far bank, give a good indication of how severe that episode of flooding was. The photograph is taken from where the Arnaud Theatre now stands.

THE LOCK c1955 G65177

MILL MEAD 1903 50880

THE YVONNE ARNAUD THEATRE c1965 G65376

The 568-seat theatre opened for its first performance in June 1965, and is named after the famous and much-loved actress who spent the final months of her life living in Guildford during 1958. The money for the construction of this irregularly-shaped building was largely raised via a national appeal launched in October 1961.

THE TOWN BRIDGE 1904 51860

The church of St Nicolas, standing beside the Town Bridge and with The Mount rising steeply beyond, was rebuilt in the 1870s on the site of the previous mediaeval church at the instigation of its then rector, the Reverend Dr John S B Monsell. He wrote 'Fight the Good Fight' and several other hymns. Work on the new building began in 1874, but Monsell was injured in a fall while inspecting the site and died in April 1875. A brass inscription on a fragment of a column in the churchyard marks the spot where he fell. The new church was consecrated a year later. The omission of the letter 'h' in the saint's name introduced what was to become a common practice in the following decade. To the left front are the premises of John Moon & Sons, timber merchants. The White House pub now occupies this site.

THE TOWN BRIDGE 1904 51861

The old stone bridge which stood here was destroyed on 15 February 1900,
when the River Wey flooded during a thaw accompanied by heavy rain. Huge
quantities of sawn timber were washed downstream from Moon's timber yard,
blocking the arches and causing the stonework to crumble. The bridge's main
arch collapsed the following day, fracturing the gas and water mains. This new
single span bridge was opened, after much wrangling, on 5 February 1902. The
previous bridge had been repaired and widened in 1825, following another
period of severe flooding. H Martin, who ran the boathouse by the bridge, was
also a confectioner and mineral-water manufacturer. On the near side of the
roadway was F Cobbett, basket maker. This bridge was demoted to footbridge
status with the opening of the gyratory system in 1972, and was finally
condemned as unsafe for vehicular traffic.

HIGH STREET 1904 51856
With St Nicolas Church on the right, and the Town Bridge just beyond, one has a clear view of the steep High Street climbing away from the river towards the tower of Holy Trinity Church; when the Guildford diocese was formed in 1927, it was to become the proto-cathedral church until the eventual consecration of the new Cathedral on Stag Hill in 1961.

BRIDGE STREET 1903 50875
Friary, Holroyd and Healy's huge brewery dominates the background. The business, originally built as a steam flour mill owned by the Masters family, was converted into a brewery in about 1868 and had flourished during the late 19th century; it acquired other smaller breweries throughout the county. In 1956 it merged with Meux Ales to become Friary Meux. It last brewed in 1969. The tower was demolished in February 1974.

STOKE BRIDGES 1906 55069
The junction of the Navigation Canal, on the left, and the River Wey at Stoke-next-Guildford, northwest of the town, are viewed from the towpath of the Wey Navigation. The imposing landmark of Stoke Mill is on the right.

STOKE BRIDGE 1906 55068
In this photograph we have a closer view of the wooden bridge, and of a little weather-boarded chapel which originally stood on what is now a marshy island between the two bridges.

STOKE MILL 1906 55067
An earlier mill stood here until 1875. The present five-storey brick structure was built in 1879; it still stands, but it is now dwarfed beneath the carriageways of the new A3 road.

Index

Abbots Hospital 32, 33

Allen's Boathouse 76

Alms Houses 32

Bridge Street 81

The Castle 44–45, 46

The Castle Arch 41, 42

The Castle Grounds 42,43

The Cathedral 66

Caxton Gardens 53

The Church of the Holy Trinity 56

Epsom Road 57, 58

Farnham Road 48, 49

The Grammar School 33, 34

on the Hogs Back 62

High Street 15, 16, 18–19, 20–21, 22, 25, 26–27, 28, 29, 30, 31, 80

The Jolly Farmer Inn 75

Keepers Cottage 66

The Lido 52, 53

The Lock 77

The Market 40

Market Street 17

The Military Hospital 47

Mill Mead 77

North Street 34, 35, 36–37, 38

Newlands Corner Tea Room 63

Portsmouth Road 58

Quarry Street 23, 24

River Wey 68, 74, 75, 76

The Royal Surrey County Hospital 48

St Catherines 70, 72–73

St Catherines Chapel 69

St Catherines Ferry 71

St Catherines Ferry Cottage 71

St Martha's Church 64, 65

St Saviour's Church 39

Star Corner 24

Stoke Bridges 81, 82

Stoke Church 67

Stoke Mill 82

Sutton Place 61

Swan Lane 39

The Swimming Pool 52, 53

Town Bridge 78, 79

Upper High Street 54–55, 56, 57

Waterden Road 50

Weston Road 51

Woodbridge Hill 59

Woodbridge Road 60

York Road 59

Yvonne Arnaud Theatre 78

Frith Book Co Titles

Frith Book Company publish over a 100 new titles each year. For latest catalogue please contact Frith Book Co.

Town Books 96pp, 100 photos. County and Themed Books 128pp, 150 photos
(unless specified) All titles hardback laminated case and jacket
except those indicated pb (paperback)

Around Barnstaple	1-85937-084-5	£12.99
Around Blackpool	1-85937-049-7	£12.99
Around Bognor Regis	1-85937-055-1	£12.99
Around Bristol	1-85937-050-0	£12.99
Around Cambridge	1-85937-092-6	£12.99
Cheshire	1-85937-045-4	£14.99
Around Chester	1-85937-090-X	£12.99
Around Chesterfield	1-85937-071-3	£12.99
Around Chichester	1-85937-089-6	£12.99
Cornwall	1-85937-054-3	£14.99
Cotswolds	1-85937-099-3	£14.99
Around Derby	1-85937-046-2	£12.99
Devon	1-85937-052-7	£14.99
Dorset	1-85937-075-6	£14.99
Dorset Coast	1-85937-062-4	£14.99
Around Dublin	1-85937-058-6	£12.99
East Anglia	1-85937-059-4	£14.99
Around Eastbourne	1-85937-061-6	£12.99
English Castles	1-85937-078-0	£14.99
Around Falmouth	1-85937-066-7	£12.99
Hampshire	1-85937-064-0	£14.99
Isle of Man	1-85937-065-9	£14.99
Around Maidstone	1-85937-056-X	£12.99
North Yorkshire	1-85937-048-9	£14.99
Around Nottingham	1-85937-060-8	£12.99
Around Penzance	1-85937-069-1	£12.99
Around Reading	1-85937-087-X	£12.99
Around St Ives	1-85937-068-3	£12.99
Around Salisbury	1-85937-091-8	£12.99
Around Scarborough	1-85937-104-3	£12.99
Scottish Castles	1-85937-077-2	£14.99
Around Sevenoaks and Tonbridge	1-85937-057-8	£12.99

Sheffield and S Yorkshire	1-85937-070-5	£14.99
Shropshire	1-85937-083-7	£14.99
Staffordshire	1-85937-047-0 (96pp)	£12.99
Suffolk	1-85937-074-8	£14.99
Surrey	1-85937-081-0	£14.99
Around Torbay	1-85937-063-2	£12.99
Wiltshire	1-85937-053-5	£14.99
Around Bakewell	1-85937-113-2	£12.99
Around Bournemouth	1-85937-067-5	£12.99
Cambridgeshire	1-85937-086-1	£14.99
Essex	1-85937-082-9	£14.99
Around Great Yarmouth	1-85937-085-3	£12.99
Hertfordshire	1-85937-079-9	£14.99
Isle of Wight	1-85937-114-0	£14.99
Around Lincoln	1-85937-111-6	£12.99
Oxfordshire	1-85937-076-4	£14.99
Around Shrewsbury	1-85937-110-8	£12.99
South Devon Coast	1-85937-107-8	£14.99
Around Stratford upon Avon	1-85937-098-5	£12.99
West Midlands	1-85937-109-4	£14.99

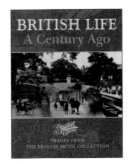

British Life A Century Ago
246 x 189mm
144pp, hardback.
Black and white
Lavishly illustrated with photos
from the turn of the century,
and with extensive commentary.
It offers a unique insight into
the social history and heritage
of bygone Britain.

1-85937-103-5 £17.99

Available from your local bookshop or from the publisher

Frith Book Co Titles Available in 2000

Around Bath	1-85937-097-7	£12.99	Mar
County Durham	1-85937-123-x	£14.99	Mar
Cumbria	1-85937-101-9	£14.99	Mar
Down the Thames	1-85937-121-3	£14.99	Mar
Around Exeter	1-85937-126-4	£12.99	Mar
Greater Manchester	1-85937-108-6	£14.99	Mar
Around Guildford	1-85937-117-5	£12.99	Mar
Around Harrogate	1-85937-112-4	£12.99	Mar
Around Leicester	1-85937-073-x	£12.99	Mar
Around Liverpool	1-85937-051-9	£12.99	Mar
Around Newark	1-85937-105-1	£12.99	Mar
Northumberland and Tyne & Wear			
	1-85937-072-1	£14.99	Mar
Around Oxford	1-85937-096-9	£12.99	Mar
Around Plymouth	1-85937-119-1	£12.99	Mar
Around Southport	1-85937-106-x	£12.99	Mar
Welsh Castles	1-85937-120-5	£14.99	Mar
Around Belfast	1-85937-094-2	£12.99	Apr
Canals and Waterways	1-85937-129-9	£17.99	Apr
Down the Severn	1-85937-118-3	£14.99	Apr
East Sussex	1-85937-130-2	£14.99	Apr
Exmoor	1-85937-132-9	£14.99	Apr
Gloucestershire	1-85937-102-7	£14.99	Apr
Around Horsham	1-85937-127-2	£12.99	Apr
Around Ipswich	1-85937-133-7	£12.99	Apr
Ireland (pb)	1-85937-181-7	£9.99	Apr
Kent Living Memories	1-85937-125-6	£14.99	Apr
London (pb)	1-85937-183-3	£9.99	Apr
New Forest	1-85937-128-0	£14.99	Apr
Scotland (pb)	1-85937-182-5	£9.99	Apr
Around Southampton	1-85937-088-8	£12.99	Apr
Stone Circles & Ancient Monuments			
	1-85937-143-4	£17.99	Apr
Sussex (pb)	1-85937-184-1	£9.99	Apr
Colchester (pb)	1-85937-188-4	£8.99	May
County Maps of Britain			
	1-85937-156-6 (192pp)	£19.99	May
Leicestershire (pb)	1-85937-185-x	£9.99	May

Lincolnshire	1-85937-135-3	£14.99	May
Around Newquay	1-85937-140-x	£12.99	May
Nottinghamshire (pb)	1-85937-187-6	£9.99	May
Redhill to Reigate	1-85937-137-x	£12.99	May
Victorian & Edwardian Yorkshire			
	1-85937-154-x	£14.99	May
Around Winchester	1-85937-139-6	£12.99	May
Yorkshire (pb)	1-85937-186-8	£9.99	May
Berkshire (pb)	1-85937-191-4	£9.99	Jun
Brighton (pb)	1-85937-192-2	£8.99	Jun
Dartmoor	1-85937-145-0	£14.99	Jun
East London	1-85937-080-2	£14.99	Jun
Glasgow (pb)	1-85937-190-6	£8.99	Jun
Kent (pb)	1-85937-189-2	£9.99	Jun
Victorian & Edwardian Kent			
	1-85937-149-3	£14.99	Jun
North Devon Coast	1-85937-146-9	£14.99	Jun
Peak District	1-85937-100-0	£14.99	Jun
Around Truro	1-85937-147-7	£12.99	Jun
Victorian & Edwardian Maritime Album			
	1-85937-144-2	£17.99	Jun
West Sussex	1-85937-148-5	£14.99	Jun
Churches of Berkshire	1-85937-170-1	£17.99	Jul
Churches of Dorset	1-85937-172-8	£17.99	Jul
Churches of Hampshire	1-85937-207-4	£17.99	Jul
Churches of Wiltshire	1-85937-171-x	£17.99	Jul
Derbyshire (pb)	1-85937-196-5	£9.99	Jul
Edinburgh (pb)	1-85937-193-0	£8.99	Jul
Herefordshire	1-85937-174-4	£14.99	Jul
Norwich (pb)	1-85937-194-9	£8.99	Jul
Ports and Harbours	1-85937-208-2	£17.99	Jul
Somerset and Avon	1-85937-153-1	£14.99	Jul
South Devon Living Memories			
	1-85937-168-x	£14.99	Jul
Warwickshire (pb)	1-85937-203-1	£9.99	Jul
Worcestershire	1-85937-152-3	£14.99	Jul
Yorkshire Living Memories			
	1-85937-166-3	£14.99	Jul

FRITH PRODUCTS & SERVICES

Francis Frith would doubtless be pleased to know that the pioneering publishing venture he started in 1860 still continues today. More than a hundred and thirty years later, The Francis Frith Collection continues in the same innovative tradition and is now one of the foremost publishers of vintage photographs in the world. Some of the current activities include:

Interior Decoration

Today Frith's photographs can be seen framed and as giant wall murals in thousands of pubs, restaurants, hotels, banks, retail stores and other public buildings throughout the country. In every case they enhance the unique local atmosphere of the places they depict and provide reminders of gentler days in an increasingly busy and frenetic world.

Product Promotions

Frith products have been used by many major companies to promote the sales of their own products or to reinforce their own history and heritage. Brands include Hovis bread, Courage beers, Scots Porage Oats, Colman's mustard, Cadbury's foods, Mellow Birds coffee, Dunhill pipe tobacco, Guinness, and Bulmer's Cider.

Genealogy and Family History

As the interest in family history and roots grows world-wide, more and more people are turning to Frith's photographs of Great Britain for images of the towns, villages and streets where their ancestors lived; and, of course, photographs of the churches and chapels where their ancestors were christened, married and buried are an essential part of every genealogy tree and family album.

A series of easy-to-use CD Roms is planned for publication, and an increasing number of Frith photographs will be able to be viewed on specialist genealogy sites. A growing range of Frith books will be available on CD.

The Internet

Already thousands of Frith photographs can be viewed and purchased on the internet. By the end of the year 2000 some 60,000 Frith photographs will be available on the internet. The number of sites is constantly expanding, each focussing on different products and services from the Collection.
Some of the sites are listed below.

www.townpages.co.uk
www.icollector.com
www.barclaysquare.co.uk
www.cornwall-online.co.uk

For background information on the Collection look at the three following sites:

www.francisfrith.com
www.francisfrith.co.uk
www.frithbook.co.uk

Frith Products

All Frith photographs are available Framed or just as Mounted Prints, and can be ordered from the address below. From time to time other products - Address Books, Calendars, Table Mats, etc - are available.

For further information:
if you would like further information on any of the above aspects of the Frith business please contact us at the address below:
The Francis Frith Collection,
Frith's Barn, Teffont, Salisbury, Wiltshire,
England SP3 5QP.
Tel: +44 (0)1722 716 376 Fax: +44 (0)1722 716 881   Email: uksales@francisfrith.com

To receive your FREE Mounted Print

Mounted Print
Overall size 14 x 11 inches

Cut out this Voucher and return it with your remittance for £1.50 to cover postage and handling. Choose any photograph included in this book. Your SEPIA print will be A4 in size, and mounted in a cream mount with burgundy rule lines, overall size 14 x 11 inches.

Order additional Mounted Prints at HALF PRICE (only £7.49 each*)

If there are further pictures you would like to order, possibly as gifts for friends and family, acquire them at half price (no additional postage and handling required).

Have your Mounted Prints framed*

For an additional £14.95 per print you can have your chosen Mounted Print framed in an elegant polished wood and gilt moulding, overall size 16 x 13 inches (no additional postage and handling required).

---

* IMPORTANT!
These special prices are only available if ordered using the original voucher on this page (no copies permitted) and at the same time as your free Mounted Print, for delivery to the same address

---

Frith Collectors' Guild

From time to time we publish a magazine of news and stories about Frith photographs and further special offers of Frith products. If you would like 12 months FREE membership, please return this form.

Send completed forms to:
The Francis Frith Collection, Frith's Barn, Teffont, Salisbury, Wiltshire SP3 5QP

Voucher for FREE and Reduced Price Frith Prints

Picture no.	Page number	Qty	Mounted @ £7.49	Framed + £14.95	Total Cost
		1	**Free of charge***	£	£
			£7.49	£	£
			£7.49	£	£
			£7.49	£	£
			£7.49	£	£
			£7.49	£	£

* Post & handling	£1.50
Book Title .... **Total Order Cost**	£

Please do not photocopy this voucher. Only the original is valid, so please cut it out and return it to us.

I enclose a cheque / postal order for £ . . . .
made payable to 'The Francis Frith Collection'
OR please debit my Mastercard / Visa / Switch / Amex card

Number . . . .

Expires . . . . Signature . . . .

Name Mr/Mrs/Ms . . . .

Address . . . .

. . . .

. . . .

. . . . Postcode . . . .

Daytime Tel No . . . .   Valid to 31/12/01

The Francis Frith Collectors' Guild

Please enrol me as a member for 12 months free of charge.

Name Mr/Mrs/Ms . . . .

Address . . . .

. . . .

. . . . Postcode . . . .

Free Print - see overleaf